GREAT WALL OF CHINA

Christine Webster
and Heather Kissock

www.av2books.com

AV² provides enriched content that supplements and complements this book. Weigl's AV² books strive to create inspired learning and engage young minds in a total learning experience.

Your AV² Media Enhanced books come alive with...

Audio
Listen to sections of the book read aloud.

Key Words
Study vocabulary, and complete a matching word activity.

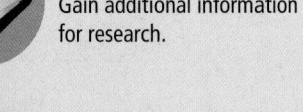

Video
Watch informative video clips.

Quizzes
Test your knowledge.

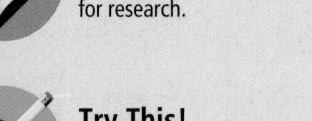

Embedded Weblinks
Gain additional information for research.

Slide Show
View images and captions, and prepare a presentation.

Try This!
Complete activities and hands-on experiments.

... and much, much more!

Go to **www.av2books.com**, and enter this book's unique code.

BOOK CODE

V442379

AV² by Weigl brings you media enhanced books that support active learning.

Published by AV² by Weigl
350 5th Avenue, 59th Floor
New York, NY 10118

Website: www.av2books.com   www.weigl.com

Library of Congress Cataloging-in-Publication Data
Webster, Christine.
 Great Wall of China / Christine Webster and Heather Kissock.
   p. cm. -- (Virtual field trip)
Includes index.
 ISBN 978-1-61913-251-1 (hardcover : alk. paper) -- ISBN 978-1-61913-257-3 (softcover : alk. paper)
1. Great Wall of China (China)--Juvenile literature. I. Kissock, Heather. II. Title.
 DS793.G67W433 2012
 951--dc23
                           2011045452

Printed in the United States of America in North Mankato, Minnesota
3 4 5 6 7 8 9 0   17 16 15 14 13

032013
WEP040313

Editor: Heather Kissock
Art Director: Terry Paulhus

Every reasonable effort has been made to trace ownership and to obtain permission to reprint copyright material. The publishers would be pleased to have any errors or omissions brought to their attention so that they may be corrected in subsequent printings.

Weigl acknowledges Getty Images as its primary image supplier for this title.

Contents

What is the Great Wall of China?

The Great Wall of China is one of the world's best-known landmarks. Winding east to west through parts of China, the wall cuts a trail through deserts, around mountains, and to the sea. Construction of the Great Wall of China began more than 2,000 years ago. It took more than 1,000 years to build. The wall is built from earth, stones, wood, and bricks.

The Great Wall was built to stop intruders from invading the country. The Chinese planned to build a wall around their entire territory. The wall was to extend through all areas where enemy forces were known to enter. It would be high enough that it would be hard to scale. Towers were to be placed along the wall so that soldiers could see great distances. These towers would be up to 40 feet (12 meters) high.

Today, millions of people from all over the world come to China to see the Great Wall. It is one of the world's major tourist attractions. In 2007, the Great Wall was named one of the **Seven Wonders of the World**.

The Great Wall of China snakes through narrow passes and up steep hilltops.

Snapshot of China

Located in eastern Asia, China is one of the world's largest countries by area. To its north lie Russia and Mongolia. Kazakhstan, Kyrgyzstan, Tajikistan, Afghanistan, and Pakistan share China's western border. China is bordered by India, Bhutan, Nepal, Myanmar, Laos, and Vietnam to its south. North Korea sits to its east. The Yellow Sea, East China Sea, and South China Sea also form part of China's eastern border.

INTRODUCING CHINA

CAPITAL CITY: Beijing

FLAG:

POPULATION: 1.34 billion (2011)

OFFICIAL LANGUAGE: Mandarin

CURRENCY: Renminbi (Yuan)

CLIMATE: Mainly temperate, but the south experiences a tropical or subtropical climate and the north can be frigid year-round

SUMMER TEMPERATURE: Average of 72° Fahrenheit (22° Celsius)

WINTER TEMPERATURE: Average of 50°F (10°C)

TIME ZONE: China Standard Time (CST)

Map

RUSSIA

KAZAKHSTAN

MONGOLIA

NORTH KOREA

Beijing ★ *Bohai Sea*

SOUTH KOREA

CHINA

Yellow Sea

Huang

Yangtze

East China Sea

NEPAL

China
- - - - International Boundary
★ National Capital

| 0 | 500 miles |
| 0 | 500 kilometers |

N

VIETNAM

LAOS

South China Sea

Chinese Words to Know

When visiting a foreign country, it is always a good idea to know some words and phrases of the local language. Practice the phrases below to prepare for a trip to China.

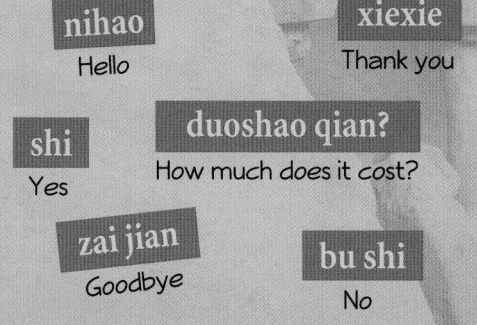

qing wen
Excuse me

nihao
Hello

xiexie
Thank you

ni hui shuo ying yu ma?
Can you speak English?

shi
Yes

duoshao qian?
How much does it cost?

buyongxie
You are welcome.

duibuqi
Sorry

zai jian
Goodbye

bu shi
No

nihao ma?
How are you?

ni jiao shen ma ming zi?
What is your name?

A Step Back in Time

In the past, southern China was ruled by emperors. The land they ruled was rich with resources. Northern China, however, was home to a group of people called Mongolians. This area did not provide as many resources as the south. The Mongolians would raid villages in the south. This often led to fighting.

To stop the fighting, China's emperor, Qin Shi Huangdi, decided to build a huge wall. He believed that the wall would keep the Mongolians out of the south and stop them from raiding his area. During his **reign**, 1,500 miles (2,414 km) of the Great Wall were built.

CONSTRUCTION TIMELINE

5th Century to 221 BC
The Chinese build small barriers along the Mongolian border.

220 BC
China's first emperor, Qin Shi Huangdi, orders the construction of the Great Wall of China as a way to defend the country against the Mongolians.

210
Qin Shi Huangdi dies. His **dynasty** falls four years later. Construction of the Great Wall slows considerably.

AD 1200s
Genghis Khan, a Mongolian leader, breaks through the Great Wall.

1368
The Ming dynasty begins. The construction of the wall continues throughout the dynasty.

Qin Shi Huangdi ruled as the Chinese emperor between the years of 221 BC and 210 BC.

Under Genghis Khan's leadership, the Mongols conquered most of northern China.

The fighting continued for many years. New emperors were defeated. Other emperors were replaced. Construction of the wall slowed until AD 1368, when the Ming dynasty came to power. The new emperor, Zhu Yuanzhang, began adding to the existing wall. The construction continued for hundreds of years. By the 1600s, the Great Wall of China measured more than 3,728 miles (6,000 km) long.

Zhu Yuanzhang rose to emperor from a modest background. His parents were peasants.

1644
The Great Wall runs from the Jiayuguan Pass in the west, past the Gobi Desert, across the Yellow River, past Peking, which is now Beijing, and to Shanhaiguan in the east.

1644
The Ming dynasty falls and is replaced by the Qing dynasty.

1644
The wall is no longer needed for defense.

1984
Deng Xiaoping, China's leader, issues orders to begin restoring the Great Wall.

1987
The Great Wall of China is made a **UNESCO World Heritage Site**. This recognition will help preserve and protect the wall.

The Qin and Ming dynasties did not call the structure the Great Wall of China. This name came from Europeans who visited the area.

The Great Wall's Location

The Great Wall is located along China's northern border. It is made up of several sections. Each one was built during a different historical period in China. The section of the wall built under the Qin dynasty stretched from the eastern part of the present-day Gansu Province to what is now known as Jilin Province. Few parts of this original wall exist today.

Other sections of the wall were built under the Han, Northern Wei, Northern Qi, and Sui dynasties. However, the Great Wall, as it stands today, was mostly built during the Ming dynasty. This Ming section begins in Liaoning Province and stretches to Gansu.

Mapping the Great Wall

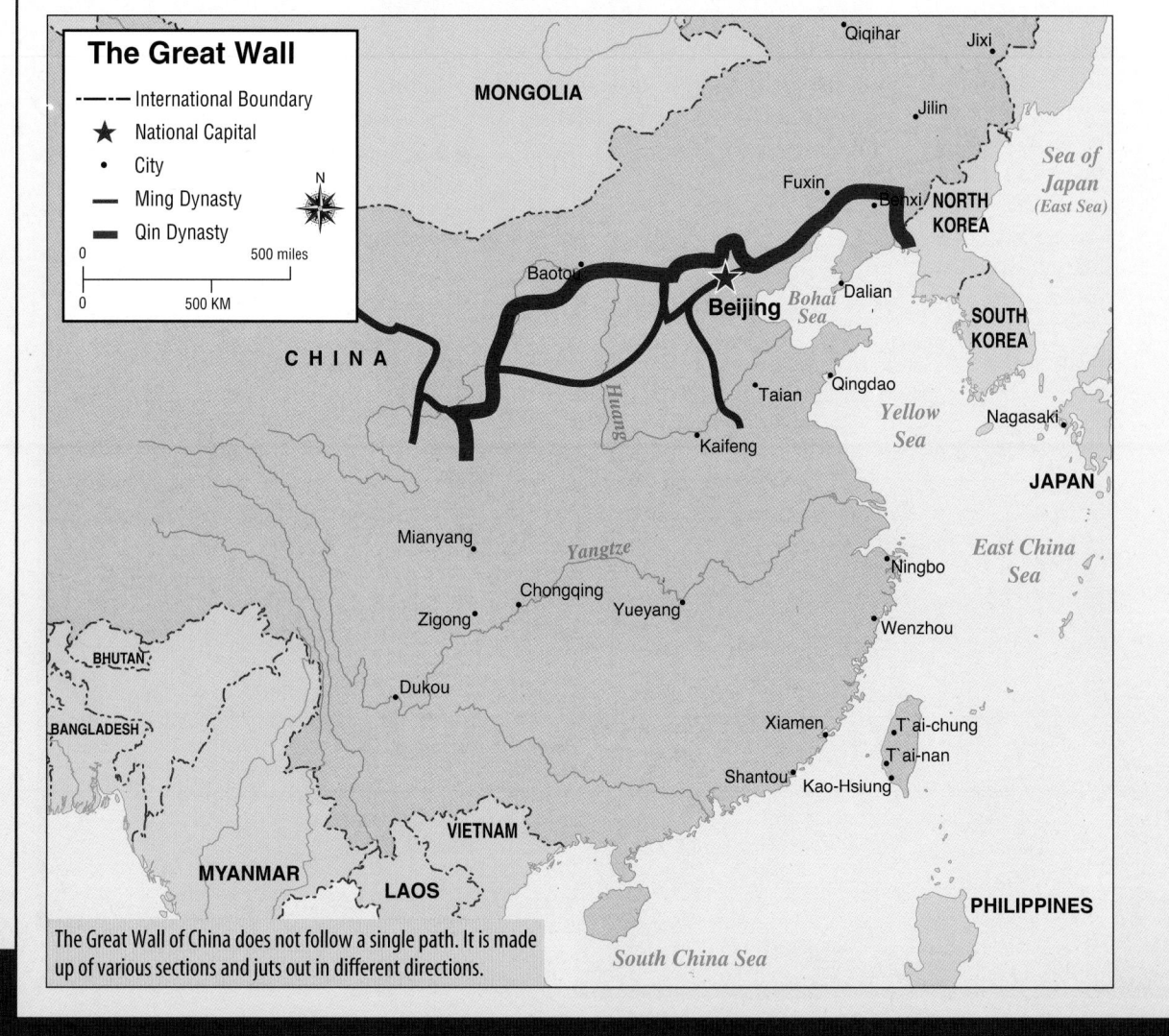

The Great Wall of China does not follow a single path. It is made up of various sections and juts out in different directions.

The Great Wall Today

The Great Wall is the longest wall ever built. No one knows the true length of the Great Wall. This is because it is so old. Some parts of the wall have been buried. Other parts have been destroyed. The best-preserved sections of the wall are found near the city of Beijing.

Length The exact length of the Great Wall is unknown. Some estimates suggest that it is 3,948 miles (6,354 km) long.

Wall Height The lowest sections of the Great Wall of China are about 15 feet (4.6 m) high. The highest sections are up to 25 feet (7.6 m) high.

Wall Width The wall ranges from 15 to 30 feet (4.6 to 9.1 m) wide at its base. The top runs between 9 and 12 feet (2.7 and 3.7 m) wide. The wall was designed to be wide enough for five horses to ride beside each other.

15 to 25 feet
(4.6 to 7.6 m)

9 to 12 feet
(2.7 to 3.7 m)

Features of the Great Wall

The Great Wall of China is more than just a wall. As a defensive barrier, it has many features that were designed to assist and support the soldiers who guarded the border.

Walls The Great Wall of China is made up of many walls. The style and materials used were dependent on the time in which the section was built and where it was built. Sections of the wall built during the Ming dynasty were made of layers of bricks. They were filled with dirt and smaller rocks. In desert areas, where resources were scarce, the wall was made of wood and dirt. Other sections were built with large slabs of rock.

Limestone, granite, white stones, and even marble are found throughout the Great Wall.

The main gate often had two parapets. One sat above the main gate, and another one, called the *weng cheng*, sat outside the gate. It protected the main gate from attack.

Passes These strongholds are found in strategic positions along the wall, often in line with key trading routes. Besides being used for trade, passes were points of access for soldiers. Each pass contains a large gate through which people could enter or exit the protected area. Soldiers watched for enemy attacks from **parapets** above the gate.

Blockhouses could be either square or round structures.

Blockhouses These towers were usually found in remote areas. They were used as both watchtowers and defensive **outposts**. As a result, they were well-stocked with weapons, ammunition, and supplies needed to wage battle against the enemy.

Garrison Towns

Soldiers who were not positioned on the wall were stationed in **garrison** towns close-by. If enemy action was reported, these soldiers could be quickly sent to the wall to help protect it.

Some Chinese communities, including the town of Zhangjiakou, began as garrison towns.

Wall Platforms

Wall platforms were a type of watchtower. They often sat level with the wall. Sections of the platform extended out from the wall. Here, soldiers would stand guard, watching for enemy activity.

Windows allowed guards to monitor the land below from inside the structure.

Signal Towers

Soldiers stationed in signal towers were responsible for sending messages to other towers along the wall. Signal towers were at least two stories high. From the top level of the tower, soldiers monitored their surroundings and reported on enemy activity using lanterns, fires, smoke signals, and flags. The lower level of the tower contained sleeping and storage areas.

Signal towers are found at regular intervals along the Great Wall.

VIRTUAL TOUR

Holes can be found along the wall. These holes are about 1 foot (30 centimeters) tall and 9 inches (23 cm) wide. They were used to aim arrows before shooting them out toward the enemy.

Key Sections of the Great Wall

The Great Wall cuts a winding path through mountains and hilly areas. Its construction created many challenges for the Chinese. Today, there are many areas that people can visit to experience the work that went into building the wall.

Jiayuguan Pass This is the first pass at the western end of the Great Wall. The pass is found between two hills. It is shaped like a trapezoid. A trapezoid looks like a rectangle with a top that is shorter than the bottom. The Jiayuguan Pass covers an area of 360,591 square feet (33,500 square meters). It was built in 1372.

The Jiayuguan Pass is considered to be one of the best-preserved military fortresses along the Great Wall.

Badaling Pass is known as the highest of all passes. It is located on Jundu Mountain.

Juyongguan Pass The Juyongguan Pass is found in the 11-mile (18-km) Guangou Valley. This pass was built during the Ming dynasty and served as both a trading post and military fort. Juyongguan Pass has two passes itself. Nan Pass sits at the south end, while Badaling Pass sits at the north end. In the middle of the pass is the Yuntai, or Cloud Platform. Made of white marble and covered with sculptures, the platform once supported three **pagodas**.

Shanhai Pass

The Shanhai Pass is located at the eastern end of the Great Wall of China. The name itself means "Pass of Mountain and Sea" and the place where the wall meets the Bohai Sea is often referred to as Old Dragon's Head. For many years, this section of the wall guarded a small pass between the northeast and central-east sections of China. The walls around the pass are 46 feet (14 m) high. Three sides are surrounded by a **moat**.

Old Dragon's Head extends for about 75 feet (23 m) into the ocean. It is said to resemble a dragon dipping its head to drink water.

Simatai Great Wall

Located about 75 miles (121 km) from Beijing, the Simatai Great Wall stretches for about 3 miles (5 km). This section of the wall is known for its steep, winding path. To reach a point called the Fairy Tower, people must climb the Stairway to Heaven, a narrow passage that rises at an 85° incline. Climbing this section is often done on hands and knees.

Simitai is one of the few sections of the Great Wall to retain its original appearance.

The tail wall, or inner branch, gave the wall a better defensive position against attackers.

Mutianyu Great Wall

This part of the Great Wall connects the Juyongguan Pass from the west to the east. It is found about 43 miles (69 km) northeast of the city of Beijing and is one of the most well-preserved parts of the wall. It measures 7,382 feet (2,250 m) long and has 22 watchtowers. The Mutianyu Great Wall features a "tail wall." This is a section that juts out from the rest of the wall.

Big Ideas Behind the Great Wall

To protect the country from invasions, the Great Wall had to have specific features. It had to be sturdy and tall. For the wall to do its job, it had to be indestructible.

The Great Wall of China has lasted through the centuries because of its builders' knowledge of loads.

Weight Loads

The builders knew that a wall of this size carried a great deal of weight. They had to create a structure that could handle strong forces and heavy loads. A load is the total weight that an object can carry. In the case of the Great Wall, this included materials and people. Packed earth was strong enough to withstand the weight of the design. The Great Wall was also designed so the bottom was thicker than the top. As a result, the broad base supports the lighter load of the narrow top.

Beaten Down Earth

When construction of the Great Wall began, workers used dirt as their main material. To make a strong wall, workers used a method called *hang-tu,* or "beaten down earth." First, a wooden frame was built. Then, the workers filled the frame with earth. With a rock or other tools, the workers pounded the earth into the ground. This removed air pockets and allowed the dirt to form a strong compact layer that would not crumble. Once the dirt was packed tightly, another layer was thrown on top. This method was repeated until the wall reached the required height.

Over time, rocks replaced dirt as the building material of choice. Rocks were better able to withstand the force of new weapons, such as cannons and muskets.

Science at Work at the Great Wall

Today, computers are used to design walls, and factories make the materials. Cement mixers smooth concrete for easy use. Bulldozers clear the earth for the foundation. Cranes lift heavy bricks to the site. This technology was not always available. The workers who built the Great Wall had to use far more basic tools.

Traditional tools are still used to maintain the Great Wall.

Tools and Supplies

In the early years of building the Great Wall, tools were limited. Bringing materials from one place to another required human effort. Thousands of workers were responsible for digging and carrying earth to the site. Often, they dug the dirt with their hands. Sometimes, they had simple shovels for digging. Woven baskets were used to carry the dirt to the site. Rocks, and sometimes wooden tools, were used to pack the earth down. If resources were far from the site or the land was steep, the workers would line up along the wall and pass the materials from one person to the next.

Simple Machines

Reaching tall heights was a challenge while building the Great Wall. Ramps of packed earth allowed workers to reach higher areas. A ramp is a type of simple machine called an inclined plane. A plane is a flat surface. When it is slanted, or inclined, at an angle other than a right angle, it can help move objects, including heavy rocks, up or down.

A ramp makes objects easier to move, but they extend the distance required to move them. Instead of lifting straight up, the items are carried or pushed over a longer distance.

VIRTUAL TOUR

During the Ming dynasty, workers mixed lime and sticky rice together to use as a **mortar** between bricks.

The Great Wall's Builders

Throughout history, many emperors commanded the building of the Great Wall, but no one person is known to have designed the structure. The wall came together due to the efforts of many workers.

Meng Tian supervised a large workforce. It is estimated about 300,000 people worked on the wall under his leadership.

Meng Tian Supervisor, Qin Dynasty

Although no architect was named, a general by the name of Meng Tian oversaw more than half of the Great Wall's construction during the Qin dynasty. General Meng Tian was Emperor Qin Shi Huangdi's military commander.

Under Meng Tian's supervision, hundreds of thousands of workers built this section of the wall. Most were forced into slave labor. Farmers were ordered off their land and onto a construction crew. Prisoners were taken out of prison to work on the wall. The working conditions during this time were harsh. The daily meal consisted of a bowl of rice and cooked cabbage. Rain, snow, and wind blew around the workers, who hauled baskets of earth and pounded the dirt with rocks for 16 hours each day. Many workers died and were buried in trenches along the wall.

Xu Da Supervisor, Ming Dynasty

In 1368, Emperor Zhu Yuanzhang ordered General Xu Da to direct the reconstruction of the wall. This work involved both additions and repairs to the existing wall. The reconstruction continued after Xu Da's death in 1385. By 1644, the Ming part of the wall stretched from Juyongguan Pass to the Yalu River, in Manchuria. Its fortifications included 25,000 towers and 15,000 military outposts.

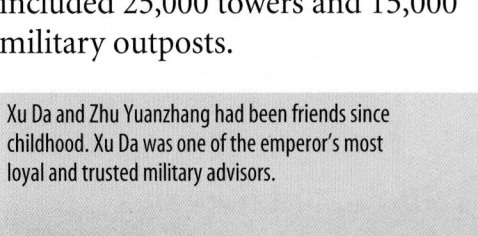
Xu Da and Zhu Yuanzhang had been friends since childhood. Xu Da was one of the emperor's most loyal and trusted military advisors.

Quarry Workers

Quarry workers cut stones from nearby quarries. They used metal **chisels** and hammers to shape the block. The heavy rock was then loaded into carts and, with pulleys, delivered to the site. Today, quarry workers use drilling machines and explosives to break up rock. Many quarry sites are located in rural areas, so workers must travel to work. Quarry work is dirty, dusty, and noisy. It takes place outdoors in all types of weather conditions.

In some countries, workers still use traditional tools to cut the rock from the quarry.

Brick Makers

During the Ming dynasty, brick makers made bricks from the materials on hand, such as clay or dirt. The dirt was mixed with water and put into wooden molds. The molds helped to shape the bricks and make sure that each brick was the same size. The molds were then put into the **kiln** and cooked until they were hard. Once cooled, the bricks were removed from the molds and were ready to use on the wall.

Bricks are still a popular building material in China. Most bricks are now made in factories.

Laborers

Laborers made up the majority of workers on the Great Wall. They were responsible for doing many tasks. They filled baskets with dirt and carried heavy rocks. They pushed wheelbarrows full of ready-made bricks to the site. Laborers continue to play an important role in construction. They perform many jobs, including cleaning sites, building concrete forms, loading materials, and operating equipment. Some jobs require special training, while others can be done without experience. However, laborers should be physically fit to do most jobs.

Laborers play a key role on the construction site. They participate in all types of construction work.

Notable Chinese Structures

The Great Wall is one of the best-known structures in the world. However, the wall is just one example of a Chinese structure. Many other ancient Chinese buildings exist in Beijing and other parts of the country.

Temple of Heaven

BUILT: 1420
LOCATION: Beijing, China
DESIGN: Ming and Qing dynasties
DESCRIPTION: This temple is used for worship. It covers 1.05 square miles (2.72 square kilometers) of land. The temple is made up of three main structures. These are the Earthly Mount, the House of Heavenly Lord, and the Hall for Prayer for Good Harvests. Each structure is used for prayer.

The Hall of Prayer for Good Harvests sits in the center of the temple complex.

The Forbidden City is a symbol of Asian culture.

The Forbidden City

BUILT: 1406 to 1420
LOCATION: Beijing, China
DESIGN: Emperor Young Le
DESCRIPTION: Today, this city is called the Palace Museum. It was built during the Ming dynasty. The city is surrounded by a wall that stands 33 feet (10 m) high and a moat. It has more than 800 buildings. In the past, people could not enter the city without the emperor's permission. This is where the idea of the "forbidden" city came.

Ming Tombs

BUILT: 1368 to 1644
LOCATION: near Beijing, China
DESIGN: Built for 13 emperors of the Ming dynasty
DESCRIPTION: These tombs were originally built for Emperor Zhudi and his wives, but they now house 12 other emperors. The main building of this tomb is 21,054 square feet (1,956 sq. m). Gold bricks line the floor. Only two of the thirteen tombs are open to public viewing.

Changling is the largest and best preserved of the Ming tombs. It is the burial site of Emperor Yongle and his wife.

Jokhang Temple

BUILT: 647
LOCATION: Lhasa, Tibet, China
DESIGN: King Songtsen Gampo
DESCRIPTION: This **Buddhist** temple is one of China's most popular tourist attractions. It covers an area of more than 269,098 square feet (25,000 sq. m). Hundreds of **pilgrims** visit here daily. They have been coming to the Jokhang Temple for thousands of years.

Jokhang Temple uses architectural features from Nepal, China, India, and Tibet.

Issues Facing the Great Wall

The Great Wall of China has deteriorated over time. Parts of it have collapsed. Some parts are about to collapse. Today, only 20 percent of the entire wall is considered to be in good condition. Thirty percent is ruined, and the rest is gone permanently. Some of this is due to the Great Wall's age, but other factors have also played a role in its current condition.

WHAT IS THE ISSUE?

Wind, rain, and sandstorms have **weathered** the wall's stone bricks.	Pollution from vehicles and factories is ruining the bricks, causing them to **erode**.	People have carved their names into the bricks and written graffiti along the wall. Some have even removed bricks as souvenirs.

EFFECTS

Weathering strips small pieces of stone from the wall. This weakens the structure of the wall.	Chemicals are breaking down the materials that were used to build the wall.	The wall's appearance is being ruined as a result of the **vandalism**.

ACTION TAKEN

Scientists are planning to cover parts of the wall with dirt to protect it. They also plan to plant vegetation in the area to restore the **ecology** of the area to what it once was.	To control the amount of pollution in the area, the Chinese government has banned any new construction within 500 miles (805 km) of the Great Wall.	In 2006, the Chinese government created a law that forbids people to do anything that harms the Great Wall. People who do so face serious fines.

Make a Sweet Great Wall

Bricks are often used to build structures. Try this activity to build your own Great Wall.

Materials
- sugar cubes
- corn syrup
- 12 by 4 inch (30 by 10 cm) piece of wood

Instructions
1. Use the corn syrup to glue one row of sugar cubes onto the long, flat side of the wood.

2. Begin gluing another row of sugar cubes on top of the first row. Be sure that the center of each sugar cube in the second row is placed evenly over both edges of the two sugar cubes beneath.

3. Continue in this pattern until you have a tall wall of sugar cubes.

Great Wall Quiz

Q What tools did ancient Chinese workers use to build the Great Wall?

A Ancient Chinese workers cleared land with their hands or shovels and lifted things using pulleys and ramps.

Q How did workers make mortar?

A They mixed lime and sticky rice together.

Q Explain the process of making bricks.

A Clay or water and dirt are mixed together. The mixture is poured into wooden molds. Then, it is baked in a kiln until it is hard.

Q Give two reasons earth was pounded after it was piled in the wooden frame.

A Earth was pounded to remove air pockets. This prevented it from crumbling later on. Packing the earth also made it strong.

Words to Know

Buddhist: of or related to the religion founded on the teachings of Buddha

chisels: hand tools consisting of a flat steel blade with a handle

dynasty: a sequence of rulers from the same family

ecology: the study of relationships between living organisms and their environment

erode: to wear away by the action of water, ice, or wind

garrison: a place where soldiers are stationed

kiln: large oven for burning, drying, or processing something

moat: a wide, water-filled ditch surrounding a fortified place

mortar: a mixture used as a bond between bricks or stones

outposts: small military camps

pagodas: religious buildings of the Far East

parapets: protective walls

pilgrims: people who journey to a sacred place to worship

quarry: a pit from which stone is obtained

reign: the period when an emperor rules the land

Seven Wonders of the World: the seven structures considered by scholars to be the most wondrous of the world

UNESCO World Heritage Site: a site the United Nations considers to be of great cultural worth to the world and in need of protection

vandalism: the willful destruction of property

weathered: broken down by the action of rain, snow, etc.

Index

Log on to www.av2books.com

AV² by Weigl brings you media enhanced books that support active learning. Go to www.av2books.com, and enter the special code found on page 2 of this book. You will gain access to enriched and enhanced content that supplements and complements this book. Content includes video, audio, weblinks, quizzes, a slide show, and activities.

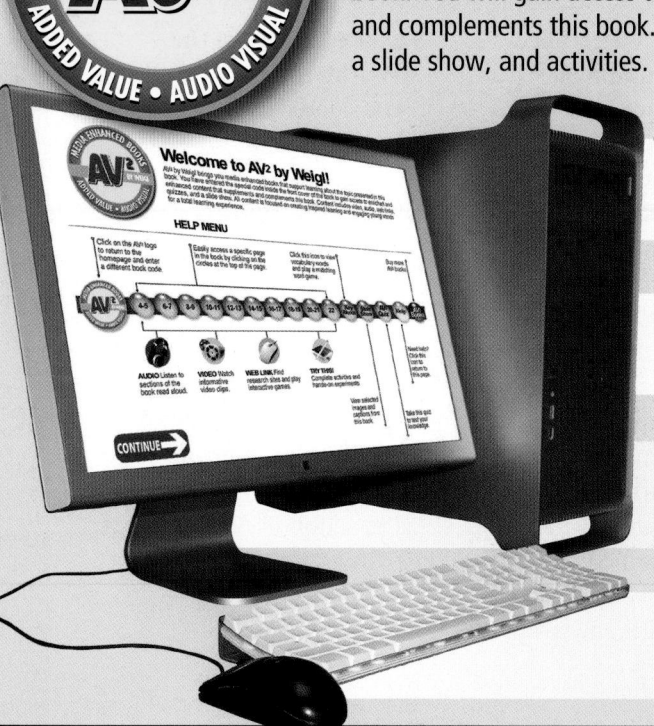

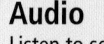

Audio
Listen to sections of the book read aloud.

Video
Watch informative video clips.

Embedded Weblinks
Gain additional information for research.

Try This!
Complete activities and hands-on experiments.

WHAT'S ONLINE?

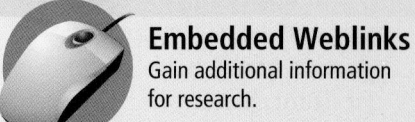 Try This!	 Embedded Weblinks	 Video	EXTRA FEATURES
Identify the features of the Great Wall of China.	Learn more about the history of Great Wall of China.	Watch a video that explains the story behind the creation of the Great Wall.	 **Audio** Listen to sections of the book read aloud.
Imagine that you are designing the Great Wall.	Find out how people are working to preserve the Great Wall.	Watch a video that follows a group of people taking a walk along the Great Wall.	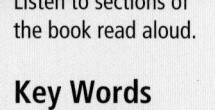 **Key Words** Study vocabulary, and complete a matching word activity.
Test your knowledge of the Great Wall.	Learn more about the different sections of the Great Wall.		 **Slide Show** View images and captions, and prepare a presentation.
			 **Quizzes** Test your knowledge.

AV² was built to bridge the gap between print and digital. We encourage you to tell us what you like and what you want to see in the future.
Sign up to be an AV² Ambassador at www.av2books.com/ambassador.